A MUCKLESHOOT
POETRY ANTHOLOGY

A MUCKLESHOOT POETRY ANTHOLOGY

At the Confluence of the Green and White Rivers

CURATED BY SUSAN LANDGRAF

WSU
PRESS

Washington State University Press
Pullman, Washington

Washington State University Press
PO Box 645910
Pullman, Washington 99164-5910
Phone: 800-354-7360
Email: wsupress@wsu.edu
Website: wsupress.wsu.edu

Publication of this volume has been made possible by an Academy of American Poets Laureate grant.

Library of Congress Cataloging-in-Publication Data

Names: Landgraf, Susan, editor.
Title: The Muckleshoot : a confluence of the Green and White rivers : an
    anthology of poetry / curated by Susan Landgraf.
Description: Pullman, Washington : Washington State University Press, 2024.
Identifiers: LCCN 2023058076 | ISBN 9780874224283 (paperback)
Subjects: LCSH: American poetry--Indian authors. | American poetry--21st
    century. | Muckleshoot Indians--Poetry. | Indians of North
    America--Poetry. | BISAC: POETRY / American / Native American | POETRY /
    Anthologies (multiple authors) | LCGFT: Poetry.
Classification: LCC PS591.I55 M83 2024 | DDC
    811/.60808979435--dc23/eng/20240126
LC record available at https://lccn.loc.gov/2023058076

The Washington State University Pullman campus is located on the homelands of the Niimíipuu (Nez Perce) Tribe and the Palus people. We acknowledge their presence here since time immemorial and recognize their continuing connection to the land, to the water, and to their ancestors. WSU Press is committed to publishing works that foster a deeper understanding of the Pacific Northwest and the contributions of its Native peoples.

Cover art by Samuel Obrovac
Cover design by Patrick Brommer

CONTENTS

PROLOGUE

Susan Landgraf

A Brief History of the Muckleshoot Tribe and the Academy of American Poets Laureate Grant

The poems included in this anthology are about searching and belonging. Loss and findings. The poets range in age, but they all share a common theme—a reaching back and a reaching forward, sometimes in the same poem.

This book is the result of a grant from The Academy of American Poets. I was honored to receive an Academy of American Poets Laureate Award in 2020. My project included teaching workshops on the Muckleshoot Indian Reservation that would result in a book of Muckleshoot poetry. After publication, a series of readings would follow, with copies of the book going to all contributors, as well as to members of the Tribal Council, the legislators from their district, and all the libraries in King and Pierce counties in the State of Washington.

The Muckleshoot Indian Tribe is a Federally recognized tribe of descendants of the Duwamish and Upper Puyallup people who inhabited the Central Puget Sound thousands of years before non-Indian settlement. Approximately 3,300 people live on the reservation with a Tribal jurisdiction covering more than 1,000 acres.

The Tribe's name is derived from the native name for the prairie on which the reservation was established in 1857. Its constitution was ratified in 1941 and is governed by a democratically elected Tribal Council of nine members.

Current members serving on the Muckleshoot Tribal Council include:
• Jaison Elkins, Chair
• Donny Stevenson, Vice Chair
• John Daniels Jr., Treasurer
• Jessica Garcia Jones, Secretary
• Virginia Cross, Councilmember
• Mike Jerry Sr., Councilmember
• Anita Mitchell, Councilmember
• Louie Ungaro, Councilmember
• Leeroy Courville, Councilmember

The majority of the Reservation is located within the city of Auburn in King County, Washington; a small portion is located outside of Auburn in Pierce County. Both the Reservation and Auburn are located near the original confluence of the Green and White rivers—rivers that held the sacred salmon and served as "highways" for the people. As Phil Hamilton of the Muckleshoot Fish Commission wrote, "We are the salmon people. For generations, salmon have sustained our way of life. Now we must sustain the salmon."

According to the "State of Our Watersheds Report" in 2012, Muckleshoot ancestors, like all Western Washington native people, "depended on fish, animal, and plant resources and traveled widely to harvest these resources." In addition, they forged ties with tribes not only in Western Washington but also with tribes east of the Cascade Mountains.

The first white outside explorers and traders reached the North and South Puget Sound area in the 1830s. In a brief war between white settlers and the Muckleshoot, as conflicts flared over land ownership, both sides suffered losses. Initially called Slaughter, after an officer by that name who was slain in the war, the town was incorporated in 1891. Newer residents disliked the name because of its association, and within two years, the town's name was changed to Auburn.

The city is the 15th largest in the State and is the site for the celebration of Veterans Day by the Veterans Day National Committee and US Department of Veterans Affairs. Top employers include Boeing, The Outlet Collection, Auburn School District, Auburn Medical Center, Green River College, and Muckleshoot Tribal Enterprises, which is the second largest employer in South King County.

There aren't many places in the United States where the first peoples have a presence as strong as in the Northwest, and especially in Auburn. Due to diseases and wars, that memory almost died out until, in the late 1900s, the Muckleshoot people set about building new lives. In the last 30 years the Tribe has built or bought a casino, amphitheater, health program, schools, racetrack, mall, and more, at the same time celebrating the land and its culture. According to the Tribe's website, the land is "tied to our heritage…What we were lasts only as long as we carry the memory."

This is a sovereign nation, where education is most important and its greatest resource is its people. I am honored that I was welcomed by Willard Bill, Jr., then Cultural Director of the Muckleshoot Indian

Tribe, as well as teachers and students at the Muckleshoot Tribal School and others. As Bill said, using the "written word to highlight our history and culture is so powerful."

I decided to order the book alphabetically by poets' last names. I did not edit the poems except to correct spelling and punctuation to make it more consistent.

I want to give special thanks to Linda Bathgate, assistant director and editor-in-chief of the Washington State University Press, for believing in this project and this book. I am honored to have WSU Press publish this book, which offers a glimpse of who the Muckleshoot are, in their own words.

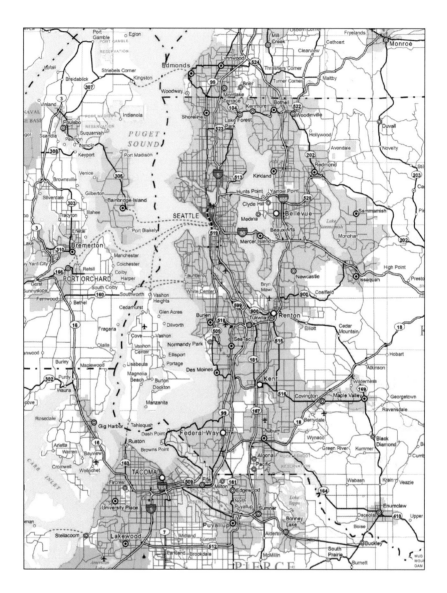

North and South Puget Sound and Peninsula map.
Map provided by the Washington State Department of Transportation.

ARTIST'S STATEMENT
Samuel Obrovac

Hello, my name is Samuel Louis Obrovac and I am a Muckleshoot Tribal Member and artist. Although primarily a painter and digital artist, I've recently begun taking an interest in traditional carving. I've previously never had any formal art training, but rather learned from the community around me. That's changed this year, and I've just started studying Northwest Coast Art at Evergreen State College in Olympia. I like to merge Southern Salish and Northern Formline styles, sometimes throwing in some contemporary styles or techniques. One of my life goals is to take my passion for art and pass that on to our future generations so our culture lives on through them.

Susan: And here's the meaning behind the "Two Eagle" book cover and the "Four Eagle" art inside the book:

I elected to use a Salish eagle since its voice is so recognizable, and thought it was fitting since poetry is a way to express one's voice. The color palette is used to represent the Green and White Rivers, in which the Muckleshoot land is situated between and used by the people since time immemorial. The two eagles symbolize a conversation, balance, equality, and duality. Some people have mentioned it reminds them of a love or courting dance. The four eagles represent the four directions, which is a sacred belief. The convergence of four eagles also represents community coming together and a shared goal being achieved by many voices.

Susan: Obrovac's other artwork in the book includes A Header Footer Design and four ekphrastic art pieces:
"CVT" inspired by Jaison Elkins' "Cowboys and Indians" poem
"Frog" inspired by Lillian Lozier's untitled poem
"I Am" inspired by Ada Marie McDaniel's poem "I Am From"
"Ponderosa" inspired by Leah Simeon's poem "The River on the Reservation"

INTRODUCTION
Susan Landgraf

As a writer and long-time teacher at Highline College, I believe writing "is an opening into oneself and one's vulnerability, which leads to a feeling of empowerment." I believe the poems highlight, as Willard Bill hoped, some of the Muckleshoot history and culture. But the poems also spotlight individuals and their personal histories, lessons, and beliefs.

I was honored to work with so many on this project. In spite of COVID-19 and the shut down; in spite of disruption on many levels; in spite of delays, this book came to be. It was an intense learning experience, one in which I came again to realize the meaning and importance of interpersonal relationships. Through Zoom workshops, and the poems that came out of those workshops and through the mail, I came to know more about individuals such as Celeste Adame, Sam Obrovac, Anna Whitefoot, Gerri Williams, Leah Simeon, Jaison Elkins, Madison Loggins, and Zip Green.

Relationships are not a means to an end—in this case a book and readings. Those relationships are an end in themselves.

Leah Simeon, who taught Juniors and Seniors at the Muckleshoot Tribal School, wrote: "We had a very exciting time with this project. The students who joined were thrilled and enjoyed their time with you." And I enjoyed and appreciated my time with them and their trust. This is where I heard the poem Cameron Williams wrote that sums up her belief in life so succinctly:

"People get knocked down / But the strongest get back up / And keep on fighting"

I am grateful to all the poets who contributed and to the following people who helped deliver this book into the world:

- The Academy of American Poets, The Andrew W. Mellon Foundation, and members of the committee that selected my proposal for a 2020–2021 Academy of American Poets Laureate grant

- Celeste Adame, who helped get word out about the book and who read at Highline College's National Poetry Month celebration in April 2021
- Lisa Amick, who teaches 6th and 7th graders at the Muckleshoot Tribal School, for inviting me into her classes
- Linda Bathgate, Assistant Director and Editor-in-Chief at the Washington State University Press, which is publishing this volume
- Willard Bill, Jr., former Cultural Director of the Muckleshoot Indian Tribe
- Trevor Bond, Washington State University Librarian, who will create a portal for the anthology and whatever else the Muckleshoot Tribe would like to include
- Dave Daley, who teaches 8th graders at the MTS, for inviting me into his classes
- Jay Hirst, Secondary Principal of the Muckleshoot Tribal School
- Samuel Obrovac, artist, who created a poster announcing the project, the cover for the book and the inside art
- Rena Priest, Washington State Poet Laureate, who wrote about the book and will take part in the book's launch
- Leah Simeon, who taught Juniors and Seniors at the MTS, for inviting me into her classes
- Anna Whitefoot, who teaches Freshmen and Sophomores at the MTS, for inviting me into her classes

Finally, I would like to give my personal land acknowledgement:

A transplant from Ohio in the early 1960s, I call the Northwest my home. I live in Auburn, on the hill above the city of Auburn, where there are mostly houses, stores, malls. My front door opens to the freeway and neighborhoods. My back door opens to the wild —trees, trees and more trees—maples, cottonwoods, cedars, pines, a pond, nettles, skunk cabbage, snakes, and coyotes. I am lucky. I know how much this King County Bingaman Pond protected area feeds my creativity. I listen to the trees talk.

I know that this land was tended by people, as Rena Priest, former Poet Laureate of Washington writes, who told stories that contained teachings on "how to live in a village alongside other people, how to live alongside the animal people, how to honor the gifts of the forests and the waterways so that they would continue to give their abundance."

With this book of Muckleshoot poems, I hope I am giving what Priest says a land acknowledgement is: "A land acknowledgement asks you to ask yourself how you can make room for these stories, and for their tellers, and for the wisdom of how to care for our garden."

I give thanks for this land and the grant I was given to bring Muckleshoot voices to the page.

CELESTE ADAME
Chasing Shadows

in the sky i found you looking   down at me
staring at cirrus clouds   basketball
bathed in sweat   arms extended
knees slightly bent   a game of one-on-one
tattered laces on shoes   2 sizes too big
socks stuffed to fit

dribble in distance grandma looks out window
better get your shoes on   i run out and we are chasing shadows
after sunset   lights turn off at dusk   our eyes adjust
hide in ditch   when we would see lights of unfamiliar cars
when we forget to duck   cops turn their lights at us
we grab cans of pop   at base of hoop
kick up ball   they follow us to your house

standing in your yard   she is yelling at us
your mom walks outside *you leave them alone*
you are 30 trying to fight 15-year-olds
we have gone out the back door when she comes in
she knows to call grandma when she is
ready for you to come home

blue and white jerseys appear
we are in middle school   practicing lay-ups
as i dribble past the hoop   into grass   fall over and cover legs
with broken cedar tree branches   you have become spinning ball on
my fingers
before movement sends it down my arm   across chest
into other hand   dribble fades

i follow you past the horizon and watch
you disappear into the tree line
my feet don't allow me to move   any further
basketball bounces in the distance   and i throw mine away
it takes me four years to pick it up   again

Medicine Creek in Four Parts
Skookumchuck

Huckleberries grow on three-foot bushes
    Cascade foothills covered with frozen mist

      first rays of sun hit open window of tent

      wake to see separation of mouths
               on each sleeping lady
          his x mark means light gathers
    is stored in locked box
next to Elliott Bay

After Commencement Bay

Because she woke before them   mountain beyond window
      shallow eyes follow through fire
         they stir in lake where she bathes
beneath hummingbirds
               teeth erupt from
child's smile.
         Because moon behind steel guard
     hair slips past palm outstretched.
Because fences do not stop me from reaching your blue curtains
      silk sheets await us
        tilt causes friction.

    Rain hits parked car

      hour falls while we sleep between black walls,
  memory is not enough to make me—

ankles itch, her foot slips from sheets.

Antelope stumbles through arroyo
constellations become soldiers pages
    seeking me out   her favorite game
ships on spider web.

Medicine Creek

for Grandpa Zug

Yellowed walls   empty spaces where pictures no longer hang

hospital bed where you drew your last breath   cowboy hat fell from
wall

                              she plays with lighter in red hoodie pocket

                    lint catches fire.

Mold grows on three week old food underneath bed.

              Brother throws bark at little sister, in frustration she

              kicks his shin

        mother grasps at chest before falling
                                        to couch, father does
not move.

Man pulls weir from White River to remove salmon

        hummingbird flutters nearby

child helps aunt pick huckleberries, one in bucket, two in mouth.

              In car, strain neck to see who got pulled over

        moon reflects off breath

their x marks were made by someone else.

Duwamish

          Wake I hear quietly. Wake. Wake.
            Before light emerges over Rainer,
            black walls bleached,
      elk drinks
   fog lifts.

You whisper into sand
          pebbles hit   fluidity of skin.

          Whisper names when you slip under surface
            emerge chilled
   run to fire beyond sands
           take from me another bucket
               start breakfast for sleeping children
           who rise with first rays.

Arroyo has not felt my presence lately
      blooming pink flower of prickly pear
         cowboy hat at bank
            smoke rings dissipate quietly
               create yellowed shadows.

Part 4, Duwamish, was published in *The Madrona Project*, edited by Holly J. Hughes and published by Empty Bowl in June 2021.

Prelude to a New Girlfriend

1.
bleeding-heart petals rub stomach   leave scent for her to follow
ruby ring waits   paintbrush sits in palette
sky is uncolored canvas left out
       a painters forgotten masterpiece

2.
way your hair falls—meteor waterfall
when sky emerges from behind trees
trails of milky way become river   leading me

back to where I told you *this is emergence*
this is where our story began to unfold—
       water map in high desert

3.
like salmon I will always return
to the base of the waterfall
       where we took our first bath
to the lake created by man
       where you told me it looked like a war-zone after the
fireworks show
to the ocean
       where I threw the basketball because I did not know what I
wanted
to water
       where words   even in their sleep   never stop flowing

this is where we *shhh* them with pursed lips and finger
leave them counting *uno, dos, tres*—

become monarch before she walks away
land on rubber band of her ponytail

a piece of parchment   and a dried-up inkwell

Something About Breath

I.

This is where   you become one with me
without the sex   where our bodies
touch one another through silence
and conversation.

I do not want this—so I am clinging to the tail end
of this galaxy where broken bottles do not exist
where promises not kept take a feather from wings
on your back—

I will tell you stories if you look into my eyes
and see reflections of constellations I have not yet named.

I will tell you stories if you look into my eyes
where you and she have changed places
and   all I want is you.

I am not begging.   I have held you
in my arms so many times   you have not listened
to the pattern of my breath   to the rhythm created
when these words   surrendered.

II.

Tonight I am your coat   your blanket
pillow underneath lower back
sheet kicked off bed
saliva rivering down your inner thigh
the hurried breath   you struggle to catch.

III.
I have created worlds past spirals, past the
planetary images, past blank spaces, past
your closed eyes, past constellations I have
painted on your ceiling.

LISA AMICK
Visitor

You found me, tucked inside
Glowing bamboo
You split the hollowed-out shell
And harbored me

I grew quickly
Our ideas, values, stories clashed
I thought I was to be
Eternally bound to your Earth
Of retaliation, rejection, hurt

And you were bound to me
A gold nugget not enough
To balance out
The pushback and misunderstanding

But now
I am finally heading to
The moon
To find self and belonging.

DONOVAN ANG
My Friend

I

Carry my friend in my arms, rushing to the hospital.

Shaken

and afraid, I can't stop the feeling of sadness spewing from my heart.

So

many emotions hitting me head on, the voice in my head saying run, run, run.

My

friend on the table bruised and bleeding, the doctors performing with speed and precision.

I

see my friend on the table not moving, I start to cry repeating sorry, come back, and I love you.

He

passed in an instant, fast as wind passing through a canyon pass.

My

only friend Ice the dog is moving to a new place, happily.

ANONYMOUS
Untitled

Home has tosses and turns
At times I feel no need to return
Concerned, I hope for better days
My surroundings feel dull, I have nothing but to gaze
Seeking every way to distract my pain, all I hope is for healthier ways
My head is scattered across my home, all I can feel is the thoughts
that roam
Although, grateful as I can be this is what I call home

ANONYMOUS
Bass Guitar

Keeping the tempo
Ibanez amplifier
Distortion pedals

ANONYMOUS
Home

Home is not a place
Home is a feeling
Home is love, joy and security
You don't need a house to have a home
Home is family and friends
Home is wherever the happiness is

ANONYMOUS

What does home mean?

It's a place where you sleep and live together.
It's a place where you can put stuff.
Playing games at home.

ANONYMOUS
Snowshoes

Awesome, great workout
We went on the gondola
Foxes eating the snow

ANONYMOUS
Untitled

My safe place is in Lakeland Hills.
A blue, yellow, white house
On the inside, there's a lot of space
I draw, sleep, and sing
Alone in my room.
My home protects me
It will always be safe to me

ANONYMOUS
Woodpecker

The top of its head is red
Its body black
Worldwide except in Australia
They peck wood, hammering away
In my yard in Enumclaw
They say nothing
I study them
A rare sight

BRIANA ARVIZU
Seasons

I am storms and rain
Made of dark skies and high winds
I bring life and death

PAUL JOHNSON-BETHELY

Home

Lake Tapps, it's home for me,
It's where I go to flee,
From the lake, Mt Rainier, is what you can see,
It's that feeling that helps you breathe,
Yesterday losing a home game vs Lutheran was very tragic,
Our team got back together, and started to make sum magic,
When I got back home, I thought of something fantastic,
Doing the work to get our team out of voodoo magic,
When I'm in the game, I started the show fantastic,
Every day I remind myself that home made this new classic

PAIGE COURVILLE
Untitled

I am Native American and honored
I want to test my limits always
I worry about being held back
I am Native American and honored
I understand that we often have to work twice as hard to get our foot
through the door
I believe the words my father says, I believe I am worthy
I dream about getting outside of my tribe
I am Native American and honored

JACK CROWELL
Untitled

In five years
I want to be in a colorful school; it doesn't have to be the biggest or
the best
it just has to be good
I like football but I don't think I will be playing it professionally
My name is Jack
I might not even go to college
But I hope I do
I don't know what the future holds
But I hope it's good

DEREK DANIELS
Basketball

Facing off against other kids
Running up and down the court
Feet pounding, heart going quick
Victorious, and undefeated
Basketball is my escape

JAISON ELKINS
Cowboys and Indians 2012

>Be Seattle
>Be summertime
>Be gorgeous as fuck
>Be a homeless Indian, in your own homeland, get shot for it
(Some luck)

That wild-wild-west, shoot first ask questions later
Never resonated with me,
All my heroes kill cowboys (Thanksgiving, RGIII)
That Lone Ranger "Justice is what I seek, Kimosabe"... kinda shit
Only embarrasses me

Listen here,
Man, if this is legit
I don't want to be
In this justice league!

"Hey, hey, hey! PUT THE KNIFE DOWN!"
(Trained to fear for his life)
40 Glock cocked, drawn, trigger finger itchin' (only The Big Duke
could have
taught this kind of swagger, this confidence)

1...2...3   4 POW POW POW POW POW, five shots
Four bullets
Rip through all he ever owned, his flesh, his blood, his bones
Tearing drunken flesh, shattering-n-splintering collagen and civil
liberties

All the same...

That one bullet that missed John...
Has police officer Ian Birk's name on it
Four bullets for the four directions Indians rev their injuns
Making as much noise as a 1000 warriors with 1000 war ponies on
the greasy

grass in 1876, this time armed with mobile devices instead of lever actions

This time we're stomping our brakes, we're fed up
Something has to be done
Injustice is not getting a free ride on the corpse of another dead Indian

Justice late is no justice
Indian time is right now
It's never all right to just bust-us
U think relics of the past, street sweep, dust us?

As tribes band together, allies from all ethnicities join the movement
Crowds grow larger, stronger, more visible, we all realize what's at stake

Just because you're poor, an alcoholic, a drug-addict, homeless, deviant, or a
minority
You don't have the power to take away my inalienable rights
As a human BE-ing, walking these streets!

Seattle, we demand a thorough investigation!
Because something isn't right
The knife you said to drop was found closed
Bullet holes mark John's side and back, we demand answers

We're all watching, we're all waiting, we're all listening

Ian Birk, maybe you should have asked questions...

Maybe he didn't hear you?
Maybe he was deaf?
How is a woodcarver holding a pocketknife in one hand
A block of cedar in the other...

Threatening your life?
He was crossing an intersection and you ran up on him, told him to

drop the
knife, gave him four seconds, then you took his life

As the questions were asked, the evidence poured out his pores,
leaking out
porous fabrics his lies were fabricated on
Unjust blood stains your hands along with your soul, so no matter
how much
bleach, counseling or prayers to god, it's un-washable

Cracks in moldy concrete are illuminated
It's a dark,   rotten reality
Business as usual, practicing patterns of illegal excessive force
He was cleaning up Seattle streets

Because if you're not paying taxes
You're leeching off society
Nobody gives a fuck about a broke artisan
Until they are dead and gone, but why not before they walk on?

Police officers are like our national military
They are the cowboys, everyone else is the Indians
All this is to say, my beef is the perpetuation of framing military
operations, as
>Cowboys VERSUS Indians<

Don't call me un-patriotic, Indians
Are over-represented in the armed forces, we love our nation, we love
our land,
we die for this shit

Even though the so-called taming of the Wild Wild West was
long ago
The code name for Osama Bin Laden was,   Geronimo

Not surprised
The U.S. just showed US, they still love to play
Cowboys and *Indians*
Now onna global frontier

Space is next...(remember Avatar?)
Na'vis, if you're listening, stand your ground and never sign any of
those treaties,
because word on the streets
unobtainium is the newest metal to make the white man go crazy

Remember Ian's bullet? Now his keepsake, to remind him of that
gorgeous day
when Indians battled injustice against the justice league.

   Today, The John T. Williams Memorial Totem Pole stands in the
Seattle Center

      Reminding all, to stand for justice, peace, for civil liberties

Solidarity for Trayvon, I throw my hood on
Stand up for the women of Juarez
Stand up for the victims of the trigger-happy vigilantes
Come together rev your injuns,

>Be heard
By sharing these words, I hope now you can see

That Wild, Wild, West, shoot first, ask questions later
Will never resonate with me
From here on out, I'm packin' heat
Here on these Seattle streets

Image: *CVI* by Samuel Obrovac

XANDER ELKINS
Night Time Guilt

The night was no different from any other, yet this one weighed heavy.
I walked through the streets, melodies hitting my ears pleasingly.
The night sky beaming down upon me.
The cold wind contrasting my warm body covered in even warmer clothing.
A car pulling up to me I felt a rush of anxiety fill me.
Every surrounding feeling and sound seemed to disappear.
My music, gone.
The cold air was now numbing and everything even felt dark despite everything still being the same.

As I walked home I felt a pit of nerves in my stomach.
The mix of guilt and fear as I frantically walked into my house and fell to my knees.
My grandmother rushing to ask me where I was.
That same night I couldn't get my nerves to calm down and barely slept.

TYLA FREEMAN
Untitled

My hand moves from right to left over a blank piece of paper,
a pencil in hand,
smudging every perfect line to make it seem blurry,
as I finish I add all the colors I can
making my canvas go from dark and sad
to colorful and bright
taking all the colors from lavender fields to orange peels
trying to make my masterpiece perfect
trying to make every color the brightest it can be from the blue skies
to the green grass

T L G
1-100 Real Quick

17-year-old mother
22-year-old father
A baby born into poverty
Life was already hard
WICC, Head Start, ICW
Now Bingo, Casino, and 12.5 housing
Parents advancing
Teens emancipating
$25-$100-$500 percaps
Trust funds and college scholarships without caps
Pills, Heroin, Meth
Never got to see where the path led
Death

Grama

Yearns for less heartache
Vows to take care of her family
Only lady I knew who loved everyone
Never missed a day of bingo
Never let her grandkids go to foster care
Everyone LOVED her

ZIP GREEN
Blackfish

In the depths of the sea,
is where you're likely to be.
You can't live without water,
so water is where you'd be.

You hear my cry in the water
I am talking to my pod. I live
in a pod. Men used to capture whales like me, like Lolita, held
captive and her cries to her pod
went unheard by them.
Nowadays I worry about capture no more.
I swim through the water, rolling and
jumping out of the water, most say I
do it beautifully. They love to see my
fins and tail.

I eat salmon and seals. They used
to be easy to catch, but lately I
am getting lazy, so my catch is
light. Also because of climate change,
there is not as much.

I am a little girl named Zip,
I dream about being this orca
because I am beautiful and love
to swim like her.

JOANNE HARRISON
Where I Came From

My cradle was once in Quinault
What an insult.
My father took me in at Quileute.
Because my mother failed the test
My father knew best
To take me to raise
I took hold of my stepmother's hand.
Not knowing my life would be grand
Her warm touch soothed my soul.
Knowing I would never have to leave out that door
Their love scorched out the need I had
To feel wanted, loved and not forgotten or
Abandoned.
At Quileute, I stand outside admiring
All the beauty around and realizing
The lost is found.

Home from the Past

Waves crashing against the shore
Whales spouting on the horizon
Rock formations jutting out of the ocean.
Sand, drift logs, campfires, hot dog and marshmallow roasts
My sister and brothers laugh as they race down the hill from the
house
The two-story house stands proudly at the top of the hill.
It holds a master bedroom and bathroom
Vaulted ceiling made of cedar
A large kitchen where wonderful meals are made.
A woodstove in big living room
3 bedrooms, rec room, bar and bathroom are upstairs
The house is always warm and full of laughter
Comfort, safety, protection.

Of Service to Others

Teach, explain, clarify
Test, test
Reteach, check for understanding
Grade, grade
Modify, build relationships
Trust, trust
Create goals and objectives
Data, data
Support in class work
Observe, observe

A Jug Full of Dimes

There it sat in front of the TV
Being stared at by my sister and me.
There was a game arcade and burger place
Not far away, waiting for us to take chase.
When our parents were gone my sister and I
Split some dimes out into our hands.
Then we raced to the arcade and exchanged them for quarters to play games.
It felt like this went on for months
Until mom finally said something.
My sister and I looked at each other and blurted out our wrongdoing.
We ended up on restriction.
Our mom laughed as she said she knew all along
Because the owner told her we were bringing in all the dimes.

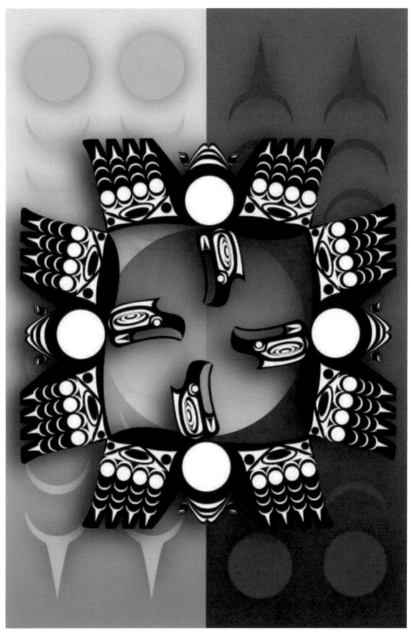

Image: *Four Eagles* by Samuel Obrovac

LASHAWNA JACKSON
Expectations

Something that I can't seem to escape, like a bird in a cage I just
wanna be free.
A burden if I can't do anything right but a dog if I sit down and listen,
except I don't get head pats or a "good girl" just another expectation
following the last.
Even bigger, almost unachievable at times but I work and work and
work just hoping next time maybe I might get something or someone
that appreciates it.

Adventures in the Night

Dark, quiet and calm. Stars shining brightly.
This is my peace and where I belong.
I walk further and further,
each step I take a breath of content leaves my mouth.
I close my eyes and breathe in the cold night air.
I like it here. I am not afraid of any monsters in the night.
I look up into the night sky, thoughts running through my head.
I wish I could stay here forever.
Alone, content and myself completely.
I close my eyes, the cold air rushing up my body and through my veins.
I belong here.
Small droplets of rain fall softly on my face
I can let all of my emotions free.
Freedom.
I long for it,
I wish to not have any restraints keeping me locked in this cage.
A sigh leaves my lips.
I look to the moon and somehow, I envy it
How it shines so brightly all alone in the night sky
How it doesn't have the restraints I do.
I wish to be just like that
But I can't and that is why I cherish my adventures in the night.

KARLEY JAMES
My Dad

My dad liked catching, holding snakes
He would look for garter snakes
put the snake on his neck and chase us
We would run away

We went on trips in the van with dad
to the mountain, to the river
We watched the deer in the field
At the river, Dad liked to fish
He would swim with us
We went to the zoo, we went camping

Once my dad broke his neck and he went swimming
when he wasn't supposed to
They had to change his cast

He liked hunting for elk
He named an elk Pedro
And he loved playing basketball
He was champion in the game

Dad loved playing Call of Duty
He liked playing hide and seek
He liked telling scary stories
Dad had good jokes that made everyone laugh

I loved watching dad do fireworks
The fireworks were pretty, and my dad wasn't sick
I miss his jokes, playing basketball with him
I wish he could come back.

HARLEY JANSEN
Untitled

I live with my parents
I consider myself an only child
The house is quiet
My mother's name is Rae Jansen
She cooks the steaks
With garlic butter and seasoning
My father's name is Errol Jansen
He peels the potatoes and mashes them
A perfect combo
They're a legit duo
I sometimes help out
We have a good time
Nothing is missing

ALIYANNA TIZNADO-JANSEN
Untitled

I want to be an esthetician and have my own spa.
When my mom was 29,
she started teaching me about skincare.
Facials, massages
A hospital-like smell, clean and essential oils.
Figuring out when the product isn't working, or when the skin is
irritated.
Products can make you break out,
but then your skin clears
People feel relaxed and comfortable.
I get to help.

MADISEN LACOUR
Where do I come from?

The place I was born? Or grew up? Or maybe live now?
The easy answer is "I'm from Washington," but if you really want to know...
I come from my parents, and my parent's parents, and their parent's parents and so on.
From my ancestors on both my mom's and dad's side.
The ones who fought for me to be here right now, sitting on my floor, writing this poem.
And the ones who probably lost their lives doing so.
But all in all, I'm still just a 14-year-old girl from Washington State.

MADISON LOGGINS
Untitled

I carry my siblings
Two live with a woman I don't know
Those siblings are strangers
Austin lives with me
We talk before we go to bed
Play baseball
And help each other with our homework
If one of us has a bad grade we give only encouragement
We do everything together
My family is supportive
There's only love to carry.

BLAZE LOZIER
What is home?

A place where you feel comfortable and safe.
A household of me, my brother, my sister, my mom.
Auburn, WA.
My favorite things to do at home is play with my dogs or play the
game and watch T.V.
Home feels like a lot of emotions. Sometimes I feel sad or happy but
as a family we get through.

LILLIAN LOZIER
Untitled

I walked in a swamp to look for a friend.
A frog sat on a lily pad.
The frog's eyes were big and upset. I went to Frog and he told me he
lost his home.
He started to sing but not a song, it was a story.
A story of his life.
At one point in his song he sang about his friend.
I asked who his friend was and he said,
"My friend is a mystery."

Image: *Frog* by Samuel Obrovac

BRANDAN MCCARTY
Dancing Toes

My son's feet, at birth his right foot was clubbed.
After NICU we had early mornings in the kitchen sink.
Cast removal, a bath, and singing to soothe my baby.

As we grew together, I remember my great grandma teaching me to
dance.
Flour on the kitchen floor, after dance practice we would practice oral
history and storytelling.
We would also split cedar bark near the wood stove.

Now as I stretch and massage my son's feet, I remember the joy I had
as a dancer.

For years I wouldn't dance or sing.
I was still, I was silent.

Best as my spent feet can, I dance with baby in my arms.
Later I will massage my aching feet.
Ease the bone spurs to be calm.
As I work my pain out, I think back to his laughter and sparkling
brown eyes.

Embracing baby close to my chest, I take a deep breath and sing the
first note in years.
I sing deep, and low rumbling voice. Soothe his tears, balm my own
hurt and begin healing my spirit.

Brown Glass

As I lie in the bottom of the bottle. Crying and wondering who
has stolen the life from me? I had only wanted to quiet my sorrows
for a little while. How did I lose nine years of my life pretending
everything was picture perfect? Where did I lose the man I set out to
be?

Drowning down in the bottle. Refilled with bitter tears of the lost
dreams. I struggle up the throat of the brown glass prison. I strangle
myself out of the opening. Choking in the freshness that burns the
stale life from me.

I am the one that threw away the years. I fed them to the bottle
demon. I gave up living until I was staring up from my casket in the
ground. I laid there wishing it wasn't true, but it was too much reality.
My spirit broken again.

All healing. Knowing I am strong enough to become human again. To
not drown myself in bitter tears caught in a brown glass prison...

Love of Old

To have love comfortable
as the faded, dried first rose.
Hanging on the wall between pictures.
The worn hall floor from all the dances.
Practiced and perfected, all the movement.

All the scars and trophies, strength and weak in all honest speaking, I
wish for our love of old.
Where chairs are pulled out, doors are opened, all things done
without being told or asked.
When love was a teamwork, two people against the world.

Starlight dinners, first movies, first kisses all under a spring ripe moon.
Wishful thinking, positive support, and team effort.
Love like a hanging faded rose, first rose captured fifty years ago.
So many years, all broken fixed and all mending done together.

All the scars and trophies, falling and standing
in all of the modern world missing love of old.
When the man did things for his lady because he enjoys her smiling.
Giving more than taking from her, balance and perfected dancing
between lovers.
Where a man was a gentleman towards his lady, at all times.

GAVIN MCCOY
Positivity and Hate

Positivity creates authenticity.
Hate, a word that can dictate.
People don't like positivity,
They focus more on hate.

ADA MARIE MCDANIEL
I Am From

I am from the precious roots of the Cedar Tree and the Pecan Tree

Both made from the precious Mother Earth of the Muckleshoot
Reservation and the precious Mother Earth of Beaumont, Texas

I am from my Native ancestors' homelands in the Cascade Range, I
am from my enslaved black grandparents of East Texas

I am from the back seat of a Cadillac car

I am from the back porch of my grandmother's reservation home

I am from the hazelnuts, baked bread, beans, soups, and stews made
from my mother's kitchen

I am from the soul food, the fried fish, chicken, neck bones, greens,
cornbread, and beans made from my father's kitchen

I am from the White River and water that were used by my mother to
wash my clothes in

I am from the wind and sun used to dry the clothes my mother
washed daily

I am from the catfish holes and bays my father fed us fresh fish from
on the weekends

I am from the red and yellow roses that I was called names from to
match my skin color

I am from the cement jungle of Hilltop, Washington, where our
mother moved us in order to try and avoid the racism of the
Muckleshoot Reservation

I am from my Aunt's foster home, where she conditioned me to know
religion and education

I am from a blended family of 10 children who my mother gave birth to, not caring what other people thought about her

I am from surviving brother and sisters who protected me from the monsters that tried coming into our home when our mother and father were gone

I am from a blended family of 10 siblings, three of whom died at very young ages, 9, 17, 22

I am from a mother who endured so much pain over the loss of her children that is considered catastrophic by the researcher. To find her nine-year-old son hanging from a tree, to receive two death notifications about her two daughters; one died from an illness at 17 years, and the second was burned to death at the age of 22 years. She is an MMIW, the case was never investigated. These deaths occurred over four years, repeating constant trauma for the entire family.

I am from survivance skills used throughout my life taught to me by my siblings, mother, father, and aunt, so that I would not become a victim inflicting more pain upon my family. I can hear my siblings still guiding me, telling me right from wrong. My father was a very special person to have met my mother with her eight children; then she had me and my brother for him to make 10. My father allowed us to remain within the Native culture with our relatives to learn the traditions and culture of my mother's people, the Muckleshoot and Yakama Tribes. I am a survivor.

Image: *I Am* by Samuel Obrovac

SHYLA MICHELL
Untitled

My family is cool, I guess
My mom is talkative
Annoyed when I take her oranges.
My dad is fun
Except when he tells me to do my chores.
The laundry sucks.
But he's fun.
I have five sisters and they are very loud
And I am not.
They're like rats fighting over cheese.
I'm going to have another little sister soon.
I don't know what her name is yet.
I wish my family was more simple.

BRANDON MORAN
Untitled

I know what i did, i tried to ignore
But no matter how hard i tried i couldn't walk through that door
I take a deep breath and step right on in and that's when my head
began to spin
My stomach turned and twisted to knots and then I began to think
those awful thoughts.
I knew what i did i knew it was bad i knew the trouble that was about
to be had
My moral compass had gone away i can't stand what i did that day
And to this day i don't forget about the trouble i caused for only sixty-
six
I tried to make up but my head says no because deep down
i'm a bad person and that's all i'll ever know

CHAD MILLAN MOSES and ARON ORTIZ
untitled

Aron play COD now
Chad let's go do that one thing
Go to the river

MORGAN MOSES
Where I Come From

I come from my grandpa.
He is kind, wise, happy and loving.
I come from Muckleshoot.
I enjoy being outside.
I don't like to test.

What Is Home?

A medium sized greenish house.
Our neighborhood is small.
Our front and back yards are green with grass.
There are trees all around.
Home is safe and quiet.

SAMUEL OBROVAC
Home

Home is where the heart is.

Home is the look in my son's smiling eyes.

Home the sound of my wife's laugh.

Home is cedar trees, nettles and ferns at my mom's.

Home is the scorching wood stove at my grandparents.

Home is the sound of the sneakers ricocheting off of the old school's gym floor.

Home is the guarantee of teasing and thickening of skin when you see certain cousins, uncles and aunties.

Home is the rushing of the rivers.

Home is the chimney.

Home is the glow of the moon in a clear summer sky on powwow night.

Home is fireworks wars with other messy haired Rez kids.

Home is just going to get gas and seeing six different people, getting hugs and a, "say hello to your mom for me."

Home is the connection.

Home is where the heart is.

Home is where the mind is.

Home is where the spirit is.

Home is where the memories bring you to.

Home is Muckleshoot.

JOHNELLE RAMIREZ (MOSES)

A Poem for Edna & Ashley

It's crazy how one day you were here, full of laughs and smiles.
Now you're gone, you left this world. Now I won't be able to see you
for a while.
I never thought I'd be saying good-bye to either of you so damn soon.
We were supposed to kick it again like we used to on Sunday Funday
afternoon.
I hung out with all three of you. You all made a point to say what's up
and show your love.
Now I'll have to talk to you through the Sun, Moon and Stars above.
I feel like you were all too young and had way too much to live for.
But you didn't see it that way.
Your hearts were broken, especially after your mom and bro left this
world. So I'll try to understand why you couldn't stay.
I know that people cry over broken hearts, but some people also die.
You were also so closely connected and bonded together, with such
close ties.
If only you could have seen how beautiful you were in your family,
friends' and my eyes.
How beautiful your hearts and souls were, your presence could lite up
any room and bring it to life.
If only I knew that the last time we'd seen each other would be the
very last, I would've hugged you longer and held you tighter.
I would've stayed close to you, talking, joking, laughing, listening to all
your stories, while you all sparked up your lighter.
But we still have all of our memories and pictures. I'll always cherish
all of the good times that we had.
Ash, I'll never forget that time we went to Leavenworth and we all
got scared and we were all freaked out so bad.
We woke up Jamie and my mom, you even called your Dad. Then we
all ran upstairs. Banson and Victoria were there too.
Or when me, you and Jamie would try to kick it at your house as teens
and your mom would always yell at us to stfu. Damn, I'm sure going
to miss you.
Edna, I remember you as always being with your sister and brother.
When one would come you were always right there.

When you got older, we kicked it a few times. And you would text me and tell me about your life.
This just doesn't really seem fair.
You were my birthday twin you would be telling me soon, it's almost Libra season, what are your plans this year.
But I know you both missed your brother and mom so much. So try to leave here in peace and we will keep your love and memories near.
Gone but not forgotten, even though your smiles are gone…
You are at rest now and hopefully you see the love you left behind.
We shall all see each other in heaven, in our dreams, and always, always remember the good times.

Sincerely, Your Cousin
Johnelle

LEAH SIMEON
The River on the Reservation

Ponderosa pine,
Sweet summer time
Mornings with coffee
And you
In our camp chairs

Sun and moon balanced on
Two ends of the river
Salmon journeying towards the home
Of the old woman
Who asked Coyote so long ago
To bring them up

Previously published in *The Madrona Project*.

Image: *Ponderosa* by Samuel Obrovac

DONNY STEVENSON
When I am an Ancestor

When I am an Ancestor and I speak through the winds to my grandchildren's grandchildren of My legacy, I hope they hear.

Creator knows, I have never claimed to be a perfect person... I have made my share of mistakes in this life. That being said, I have learned and grown from every one of them and tried to live my life by simple principles each day. Be a good person. Help those that I can. Always try my best. Speak and act with honesty and integrity. Treat others with respect and
dignity. Always look to understand before being understood. Always love and never hate. Leave everything better than you found it. Appreciate every opportunity, chance, and second chance life provides.

When I am an Ancestor and I speak through the winds to my grandchildren's grandchildren of Our People's legacy, I hope they hear.

We come from a people of warriors and leaders, of teachers and healers, of providers and care-takers. Our proud culture and identity have persisted for thousands of years and through literally hundreds of generations... since time immemorial. We carry with us the teachings and traditions of all those who came before. To also do so, to in fact carry this proud cultural identity forward, is a profound responsibility that must be fulfilled. Conversely, these teachings and traditions are a living force within each of us. They define us. They carry us and provide our foundation. This is a gift of the highest honor.

When I am an Ancestor and I speak through the winds to my grandchildren's grandchildren of Their legacy, I hope they hear.

I will tell them every day I lived and every decision I made was done to honor them and to hold them up. How I lived to carry the teachings of our shared history into the future they represent, acting as a bridge so that the connection remained unbroken. I will tell them that even though I knew we'd never meet, I loved them and had them and their best interest in mind and in heart every day of my life. I will tell them, to do so is who we really are and who Creator intends us to be. I will tell them they are strong. I will tell them they are proud. I will tell them they are Indian. I will tell them it is now their turn to do the same. I will tell them:

When You are an Ancestor and You speak through the winds to your grandchildren's grandchildren of their legacy, You will hope they hear.

Image: *Circle* by Donny Stevenson

RICKYLEE THOMPSON
New Memories of Me

Lucky man posing as me in your mind.
The man I used to be.
The memories of me.
He is gone now.
It's time for you to say goodbye to that man. Posing as me.
Look at me now.
I am new.
I am happier more gentle and kind.
That man you knew before wasn't who I was meant to be.
So if you can forget that guy
posing as me
see me now.
This is who I am meant to be.

I have lived, I have grown wiser.
That guy you see in your mind was selfish and mean.
I have faced death at my door.
I have new eyes to see this world in.
My heart broke because of that man.
The one in your mind.
The memory of me.
He was foolish.
He hurt not only you but me.
I'm happy he is gone,
wish you would forget who he was.
I'm a new memory to build now.

So you can say goodbye to that man
in your mind posing as me.
That's what I used to be.
The memories of me.
Let this man standing here.
be the lucky one to be in your mind.
The new memories of me.

The Witness

I sit there in my suit with my back aching.
Listening to my mother tell a story.
A story of her sister who had just passed.
As she speaks she breaks down in tears.
I feel I should stand up and walk to her for comfort.
In that moment I find my knees shaking
wondering if I should run to her
or keep the position of respect for our auntie who has passed.
I watch as my baby sister steps up to comfort our mother.
As I see tears running down their faces
I break down and cry for them.
My soul leaves me.
My body empty, my mind telling the rest of me to stay strong.
But how can I not feel the pain my mother is feeling
in that moment
as she cries out my sister.
An image came into my mind as if that was my sister laying there.
I could never be as strong as my mother, my auntie and my uncles
were,
As they lay their sister to rest
I pray I'm first to go.

Addiction

I stood there for what felt like hours.
Looking into a stranger's eyes.
Listening to his stories
without his lips moving or a word being spoken.
He smiled when I smiled, laughed when I laughed.
In my heart I felt his pain so deep it cut.
He cried when I cried.
Sent chills through my skin and down my spine.
I realized the stranger I was looking at
was me.
Even knowing this,
he kept looking deep into me
seeing a man that once lived free.
How dare you judge me!
I screamed.
I fell to tears as I watched this man falling to his knees.

Take Us Back

Take us back to our innocent days
sitting on a log playing in our childish ways.
Not a worry in our mind but how the Army man will survive.
The imagination we had kept our minds blind to this world
allowing us to be free.
When a rock wasn't a stone, but a ship, we can skip along the river's
skin.
A stick wasn't just wood but a rifle we used to keep the enemy away.
Take us back to our innocent days.
Looking at the night sky with all the adventures within the stars
above us.
Sitting in the grass as we watched the colors of the fancy dancer's
dress change.
Tapping our feet to the drum's beat.
Take us back to that laughter as we stomped in the mud.
Bring us back to the times we would lay our heads on our mother's
shoulder,
as we listened to our elders teach
slowly falling asleep.
Take us back to our innocent days, where falling in love didn't end in
pain.
Puppy dog eyes for the girl next door.

Our Elder Speaks

As she stands and begins to speak,
I listen.
As she talks, she begins to cry.
I cry with her.
The story she had to tell to us,
the youth of her generation,
the experience of her life and loss of loved ones.
She is celebrating a birthday
with her family.
What's on her mind is a family in our tribe
mourning the loss of their family member
leaving behind young ones.
She cries for them.
On her birthday
I see this and I feel her pain.
To have an elder to teach you of their past is an honor.
To be that elder to share what you know
is to remember the pain you have had to endure.
Today I've learned how truly blessed I am to have such elders to teach me.
My hands go up to you.
Thank you for giving me the opportunities I have in my life.

TRINITY ULRICH
Untitled

I am a Muckleshoot Tribal member. I come from Oakville, Washington. I lived there until I was 5 years old. I moved to Auburn in 2011 with my parents Eric and Rosie Ulrich. They grew up in Oakville, Washington; this is where our family is from. We come from the Sanders family in the Chehalis Tribe; we lived on that reservation. I am from the Starr/Baker family from Muckleshoot. I come from the James family in Quinault. My parents moved up here to give me a better life than what was offered to me in Oakville. I am glad that my parents made the decision to move up here; there are so much more opportunities as a Muckleshoot Tribal member when you live within the reservation radius. I get to attend Muckleshoot Tribal School, which is a godsend. My parents went to public school and I hear it was horrible for my mom as an indigenous person.

I come from a strong Shaker family on both sides of my family. I do not know the Shaker religion but I know my mom prays for us in the Shaker religion. Where I come from everybody knows everybody; everybody calls you cousin or friend. It is not like that up here. When I go back to my hometown I always feel welcomed like I never left. Oakville/Chehalis Tribe is a great community to grow up in, family friendly and lots of stories from the elders.

I cannot wait to go back to my hometown this summer to see my family and friends; that is where all my aunties and uncles are.

KYLA VALLES
Untitled

A bright green leaf
with big water droplets
Smooth texture
Going down a stream
Calming
Travelling where the water goes

ISADORE VAN BRUNT
Polar

My Dachshund, Polar
Was he shy or guilty?
We thought shy, until we discovered it was
guilty.
He would lower himself to the ground and drop
his ears.
The guilt set in.
Why?
Because there were puppy pads everywhere,
but no piddles on the pads.
The piddles were hidden all around the house.
Poor Polar.
We said, no, no, no!!
He said love me, love me, love me, with a wag
of his tail.
With a quick pat on his head, he slipped away
Under the door and continued being a sweet,
carefree puppy.

KRISTAL VEJAR
Anger

I can't control it, doesn't matter how hard I try.
It controls me in the end, to my actions to thoughts.
It makes me see red, a soft white noise in my ears.
It heats me up, makes me feel suffocated.
I don't mean to yell.
I don't mean to hurt you.
I'm sorry, please don't hate me for this.
I try to rein it in, but it controls me.
It always does in the end.
        Anger

SARIAH WALDEN
Home

Home is the gym I go to for practice
The sound of basketballs dribbling, hype music
Shoot, dribble, pass the rough orange ball
Coach Smith makes our drills like games
In sync with my teammates
I feel happy and hot with sweat
The gym is where I achieve my goals

TROY WHITE EAGLE
The Life of Troy

My grandparents and my auntie raised me growing up. I grew up uptown.
Some defining memories would be cooking with my grandma Regina and baking with my auntie.
I want to accomplish getting better at wrestling.

ANNA WHITEFOOT
Haiku

Muckleshoot Tribal
School has the best kids around
Laughter every day

CAMERON WILLIAMS
Haiku

People get knocked down
But the strongest get back up
And keep on fighting

Where do you come from?

I am Navajo and Muckleshoot.
I grew up in Muckleshoot.
Every year I went down to New Mexico so I could see my family.
A memory I have is getting in a canoe the first time.
I try to go down to my ancestors' roots so I joined the Muckleshoot
Canoe Family.
I wanted to live in New Mexico with my grandma but she passed.
I'll miss my grandma but I'll always think positive thoughts about her.
Like when we always go down to the flea market and get stuff.

GERRI L. WILLIAMS
Ghosts of a Crystal Page

Although sound is hushed by strawberry lips
stitched through the hands of a crystal mime,
      where an albino blue jay sips raspberry vodka
      through white chocolate truffles,
      blows turquoise glitter
      in Whulsootseed air-

      it is another part of me:

A shattered porcelain clown nose,
      a sunflower music box on indigo shelves.
      A voice message from Clarence in my diary,
      an ant crawling out of cement
      not yet dry.

When three crowns framed on espresso walls drip
      nappy dreads on New York streets.

When holiday love songs
      are broken halos
      placed in a sesame street garbage can
      next to a Miles Davis CD.

When a crisp bottle reveals
      pink conversation hearts in clear waters,
      I let them melt on my tongue –

They trickle between sugared lips, drooping
      into empty pages,
      climbing through bullet hole windows,
      following ghosts of little children
      chasing chocolate chip dreams.

A Red Skin Girl bathes in lyrics of Bob Marley,
      kissing saltwater trickling
      upon his cheek.

Old letters become whispers of ash between her fingers,
     mascara lines painted
     in a trembling line.

Lavender moon brings a peppermint wand
     to her pink frosted lips: *ssshhhhh.*
     No Woman. No Cry:

Leave it for your brother with tattoo ink glistening
     from midnight pupils.

Leave it for the wind
     that gives life to broken windows.

Leave it for the porcelain clown sleeping
     in the midst of drooping eyes.

Let Love Spell lather her voice into your body,
     violet bubbles tracing summer night blues.

Let the *Puyallup* boy sprinkle sand into the crease of winter pages
     only ghosts of the *Bəqəšut* people can read.

Let me sprinkle a new snow over the Muckleshoot earth.

Leaves in October

1.

I was born into light at sunrise; the hollow between a seashell, *keye*, a ghost-like reflection washing my body with cedar boughs from Green and White Rivers; soil from Black River upon my feet.

Her voice pressed into my fingerprints – white woven blanket against my skin. Abalone buttons and clamshells sewn into grandfather's story around me: A. Williams from the Puyallup Tribe.

Mother, watching J.P. Patches, the local TV clown show, was a woman who comes from Muckleshoot and Puyallup waters, a woman of sockeye People and white candle prayers.

My father, a collection of onyx underneath cattails along Puyallup River, born from Umatilla beaded stories and smoke from salmon flesh.

He is the white of my woven blanket, not the fabric against my skin – the white of my seashell, the forest green of abalone – my first breath in October.

2.

Leaves glazed with pumpkin and cinnamon drifted along White River, stumbled between sandstones, coasted like the ghost of a Muckleshoot girl who once lived along those banks, drifted like *si ? sXeb* on old Muckleshoot highways.

They tumbled underneath the sun into a den where a wolf child was born with red clay upon her cheeks. As crow sang from Redwood, as Chinook returned upstream, as leaves fell before *stiqayu?*, together, we opened our eyes.

Author's note: Keye means Grandmother. si ? sXeb is the name of my canoe song which came to me on the water in the summer of 2005. It means when an adult lightly pounds a hand drum a child will get up and dance. stiqayu? means wolf.

The Whale

from 3rd grade

I saw a whale out in the sea one day.

I looked at him.

He looked at me.

We looked at each other all day.

My eyes got tired.

The whale's eyes got tired.

So we went to sleep.

When I woke up

the whale was gone—

so I began to cry.

The whale came back.

I gave him a hug.

And then I told him bye.

KAI WILLIAMS
Untitled

I carry my memories of New Mexico
I live in Auburn, WA on the reservation
Most of my mother's family lives in New Mexico
Dry heat, wheat colored land
Talk about what I'm doing, how I'm doing
I see the protective nature of my family
Wanting us to be careful of what we do
Teaching us life skills
Cleaning the house, making sure we exercise
Teaching us the Navajo language
A family of many personalities
I feel safe

NICHOLAS WILSON
Home? What is home?

Home is where I feel comfortable and relaxed,
home is a place where you can feel safe and comfortable.
One thing I love to do at home is talk to friends and chill.
Family is home.
Home smells like Neala's spaghetti
It sounds like kids yelling
Yakama and Puyallup flags above the door
Xbox's buzzing
Victor, Charlie, Nina chillin'
My home.

AUTHOR BIOGRAPHIES
(as of May 2021)

Celeste Adame, Muckleshoot, has been published in the *Santa Fe Literary Review, As/Us: A Journal for Women of the World,* and numerous Institute of American Indian Arts anthologies. She holds a Master of Fine Arts in poetry from the Institute of American Arts in Santa Fe, New Mexico.

Lisa Amick is a Japanese American teacher at Muckleshoot Tribal School in Auburn, WA. She loves her students and embraces the opportunities and challenges that teaching brings. Lisa enjoys hiking, baking, reading, and creating art. She is an aspiring writer, and would, one day, love to publish a book.

Donovan Ang is a student at the Muckleshoot Tribal School.

Anonymous is a student at the Muckleshoot Tribal School.

Anonymous is a student at the Muckleshoot Tribal School.

Anonymous is a student at the Muckleshoot Tribal School.

Anonymous is a student at the Muckleshoot Tribal School.

Anonymous is a student at the Muckleshoot Tribal School.

Anonymous is a student at the Muckleshoot Tribal School.

Anonymous is a student at the Muckleshoot Tribal School.

Briana Arvizu is a student at the Muckleshoot Tribal School.

Paul Johnson-Bethely is a student at the Muckleshoot Tribal School.

Paige Courville is a student at the Muckleshoot Tribal School.

Jack Crowell is a student at the Muckleshoot Tribal School.

Derek Daniels is a student at the Muckleshoot Tribal School.

Jaison Elkins is Chair of the Muckleshoot Tribal Council. He is from the Moses, Dominick, Starr, Barr, and Elkins families. He has a BA in Political Science from the University of Colorado Boulder, an AA in Native Studies from Northwest Indian College, and a high school diploma from Auburn High School.

Xander Elkins is a student at the Muckleshoot Tribal School.

Tyla Freeman is a student at the Muckleshoot Tribal School.

Tammy James Gourdine has four biological children and has fostered many others. She is a Muckleshoot Tribal member who has lived in Muckleshoot her entire life. Her father's tribe is Yakama Nation. She has an MBA in Community Economic Development and loves learning and writing.

Zip Green is a student at the Muckleshoot Tribal School.

Joanne Harrison is a paraeducator at the Muckleshoot Tribal School.

Lashawna Jackson is a student at the Muckleshoot Tribal School.

Karley James is a student at the Muckleshoot Tribal School.

Harley Jansen is a student at the Muckleshoot Tribal School.

Aliyanna Tiznado-Jansen is a student at the Muckleshoot Tribal School.

Madisen LaCour is a student at the Muckleshoot Tribal School.

Madison Loggins is a student at the Muckleshoot Tribal School.

Blaze Lozier is a student at the Muckleshoot Tribal School.

Lillian Lozier is a student at the Muckleshoot Tribal School.

Brandan McCarty is a visual artist and writer inspired by life around him. He is a Makah Member, residing within Muckleshoot. He has been involved in writing and art since the age of five.

Gavin McCoy is a student at the Muckleshoot Tribal School.

Ada Marie McDaniel is from the Muckleshoot and Yakama Tribes. She is a survivor.

Chad Millan Moses is a student at the Muckleshoot Tribal School.

Shyla Michell is a student at the Muckleshoot Tribal School.

Brandon Moran is a student at the Muckleshoot Tribal School.

Morgan Moses is a student at the Muckleshoot Tribal School.

Samuel Obrovac is a Muckleshoot Tribal member and self-taught artist.

Aron Ortiz is a student at the Muckleshoot Tribal School.

Johnelle Ramirez (Moses), Muckleshoot, has a daughter and a son. She has a Bachelor's in Technical Management, specializing in Project Management; an Associate's in Native American Studies; and a Certificate in Tribal Gaming and Hospitality Management. She enjoys spending time with family and friends, music and poetry, ballroom dancing and being in nature.

Leah Simeon is a citizen of the Spokane Tribe of Indians. She worked at the Muckleshoot Tribal School in Auburn, WA, as a high school English teacher. During her time at MTS, she loved hearing student stories about going to the river, powwows, and up to the forest.

Donny Stevenson is a carver and painter. He's also vice chair of the Muckleshoot Tribal Council and a member of the Indigenous Advisory Committee. He earned his BA from the Evergreen State College and is passionate about accessing the traditional teachings and wisdom of the ancestors and elders.

Rickylee Thompson is a single father who writes poetry as self-therapy to cope with a difficult past.

Trinity Ulrich is a student at the Muckleshoot Tribal School.

Kyla Valles is a student at the Muckleshoot Tribal School.

Isadore Van Brunt is a student at the Muckleshoot Tribal School.

Kristal Vejar is a student at the Muckleshoot Tribal School.

Sariah Walden is a student at the Muckleshoot Tribal School.

Troy White Eagle is a student at the Muckleshoot Tribal School.

Anna Whitefoot is a daughter, sister, and auntie. She is a Yakama Tribal member. She's a Zag and a Coug. She's an Indigenous educator at the Muckleshoot Tribal School and says, "My high school students are the best! I am so proud of their poems and hard work."

Cameron Williams is a student at the Muckleshoot Tribal School.

Gerri L. Williams has been writing poetry since she was four years old. She knew her whole life she was going to be a writer and a poet. She attended The Institute of American Indian Arts and earned an AFA in creative writing. She wants to write about her survival during times of hardship and a collection of poetry about her time at Standing Rock as a Water Protector.

Kai Williams is a student at the Muckleshoot Tribal School.

Nicholas Wilson is a student at the Muckleshoot Tribal School.

ABOUT THE CURATOR

Susan Landgraf's chapbook *Journey of Trees* will be published by The Poetry Box in May 2024. *Crossings* was published by Ravenna Press as part of its Triple series #17 in 2022. She was awarded an Academy of American Poets Laureate award in 2020, which resulted in this volume.

Other books include *The Inspired Poet* from Two Sylvias Press (2019); *What We Bury Changes the Ground*; a chapbook titled *Other Voices*, and *Student Reflection Journal for Student Success* published by Prentice Hall. More than 400 poems have appeared in *Prairie Schooner*, *Poet Lore*, *Margie*, *Nimrod*, *Third Wednesday*, *Calyx*, *Rattle*, and others.

Landgraf has given hundreds of readings and workshops, including the Port Townsend Writers' Conference, the San Miguel Writers' Conference, and the Marine and Science Technology Center, in the United States and abroad.

A former journalist, she taught at Highline College for 30 years and at Shanghai Jiao Tong University in 2002, 2008, 2010, and 2012. She served as Poet Laureate of Auburn, Washington, from 2018 to 2020.